a compound of words

a compound of words

Fióna Bolger

YODAPRESS

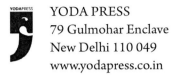

YODA PRESS
79 Gulmohar Enclave
New Delhi 110 049
www.yodapress.co.in

ISBN 9789382579755

Editor in charge: Tanya Singh
Typeset by Dharambir Singh
Printed at Replika Press Pvt. Ltd.
Published by Arpita Das for YODA PRESS

Even as he falls shattered
like twigs from a nest undone
he feels
that everything could be set right
with a poem

—'With a Poem' by Perumal Murugan
(trans. Aniruddhan Vasudevan)

CONTENTS

ACKNOWLEDGEMENTS

Thank you to the editors of the following magazines and books in which some of these poems, or versions of these poems, have previously appeared: *Bare Hands Anthology, Flare, Poetry Bus, The Brown Critique* and *Wretched Strangers.* Thank you also to Peadar and Collette O'Donoghue for allowing me to republish work from *The Geometry of Love Between the Elements* and *Triptych.*

My sincere thanks to all who read and critiqued this collection, especially Anne Tannam, Margaret Dee, Özgecan Kesici-Ayoubi and Tapasya Narang. To my fellow poets and dreamers, the clusters of writers to be found in Dublin Writers' Forum, Airfield Writers and Rathmines Writers' Workshop, who have helped these words find their form. To K. Srilata and Alvy Carragher for their transnational support and encouragement.

To Jackie and Jim, Lakshmi and TRG, and all my family and friends everywhere, thank you for your love and kindness. And to Liadán, thank you for being you.

To Arpita Das, Tanya Singh and the rest of the team at Yoda Press for polishing up these words and letting them shine, diyas in darkness.

a compound of words

try to atomise wajalukinat
imagine each letter a string supplying
a side way to transubstantiation avoiding
the black hole of a lemon market
the consonants shifting, the click of the q
celtic fossils trickle down through the generations
d'ya know it's all maya and we,
saala, must do penance
aadivanga knee as you cruise for a bruise—
crushed together we make juice

Coarse Outline

I remove my skin
pin it with wooden stakes
near the Liffey
to dry in the sun.

With tanner's lime
I prepare it for writing

I take cow dung mixed with water
to form a pure black ink
and write myself.

When the writing is done
I wrap the skin around me
my words, incantations
protecting me
against those who say
it is not so.

Wattle and Daub

Words to me are incantations
talismans held aloft against
those who say it is not so.
They form a wattle and daub fence
against my attackers.

From the coppiced wood
I choose each hazel rod carefully
I sharpen one end to a spike
jab it deep into the ground.

I weave willow wands
still moist from the river side
to form a web, then the earthing
to ground my fence.

Bare hands gather soil and straw and dung
a child's mud cake to daub my adult frame
soft and flexible yet strong against the wind.
I am protected.

An accidental flame does not
destroy my wall but hardens my resolve
with time I realise the danger from fire,
from damp, from wind, from rain.

My strength becomes my weakness
I choose silence under an oak.

Off Course

brown backed notebooks fed to the fire
as the steam roller chugs along
East Coast Road, looming higher
than its shiny chested servants
rushing round in ragged lungis
attending to the monstrous
machine's every need

they have already razed
the houses, shops, illegal extensions
built claiming a better life
inside walls exposed
a Ganesh tile observes
his failure—the wrong
obstacles removed

smoke billowing from the warm tar
the workers' feet swell
in rubber boots
as they walk the hot coals

I sit naked ash covered
smoke swirling on the ghat
my hair matted
my cup a skull
as I search
for rags and bones
among the ashes.

Pattambuchi

I walk the streets with scissors
grasped in my pocket
I lop chunks of fabric off discarded
inside out and broken umbrellas
my plan is to sew the pieces together
coat them with a waxy fantasy
then using old belts attach my willow basket
and climbing in I fly away

in my dreams

               the balloon bursts

each patch

               becomes a pattam

and I'm borne aloft

               by butterflies.

Rasika I

There are words that stick
between my teeth. Do they show
when I smile, phrases caught
from others' languages, recipes
from others' families, masalas
made in others' kitchens? Can you smell
them on my breath, or as you enter
my home? Do you want to see where
I have written them in notebooks
marked them on jars? I whisper
them in my daughter's ear,
the essence of who we are.

Biting my Tongue

My teeth close, a portcullis on my tongue.
I am reminded of the price of protection.

Pappamma kept her drunken man
as defence against his tribe.

Men recognise some limits
those set by other men.

View through the Crack

I want to part myself
crack open and reveal

Kanchenjunga in the morning sun
Topslip in dappled green midday light
Bay of Bengal moon path out to sea

mounds of coloured beads on white tarpaulin
sacks of sorted waste outside red brick houses
children dancing in overflowing water

hot sambhar on soft rice with melting ghee
Heera Halwai's earthen pot of gulab jamun, warm, sticky and sweet
thick creamy curd or Hospet Rajasthani khoa with whole black peppers

but I am afraid
how to push the images back in
seal the crack

my mouth waters
I swallow
keep it in
hold it back.

Oranges are not the only fruit

have you tried mangoes in May
hottest month sweetest fruit
warm from the day's heat

lengra long and thin
bite the skin
suck out the juice

alphonso golden breast
dripping honey
devour whole

plump banganapalli
pedestrian perhaps
but the right one is delicious

in Santhi's hands
perfect cubes of orange
forked from glass bowls

overeager fingers
rip skin dribble juice
teeth hit hard stone

Words to a New Wife Entering her Kitchen

Pack away your feelings neatly in spice jars
carefully label each one, clearly in black.
Anger first you pack with chillies, red and hot
manjal will fight off all sickness, even lust
cloves, levang, take away pain, let go your hurt
cinnamon sweet spice of joy, leave friend love here.
Jeera next, reduces pain of birth, put away child love.
With saffron your baby can come fair or not at all, store control.
Asafoetida, stinking spice, will hide shame
black pepper, currency once, conceals your greed
saunf's sweet taste helps digest disappointment,
happiness can be kept here.
With menthia, fear of age, fear of life,
bitterness will go unnoticed.
Whatever heats your blood, ginger won't reveal it.
Memories pack away with ghusa ghusa, forget.
And when you finish scattering yourself around your kitchen
do not be surprised if you think like a cabbage
dream of beetroot and aspire to be grain.
You are now vegetable matter, no longer fruit.
Only raw mangoes come in the kitchen.
The ripe and juicy maambaram are eaten at first sight.

What am I?

namak

I am salt
hard crystal form
dissolving in you

chinni

I am sugar
crushed from cane
purified for pleasure

lal mirchi

I am chilli
you are burned
by my touch

yashtimadhu

I am liquorice
sweeter than sugar
I set your pulse racing

dal chinni

I am cinnamon
from the tropics for winter
as sweet and hot as you wish

Rasika II

Her first taste of food licked
from a fingertip then sucked
hot and sour and salt, rasam.

Her chubby body knows
goodness, senses fresh
to this world, already a rasika.

Aubade

Between waking and rising
there is only a moment.

Mat rolled, pillow stashed
the woman bathes and knots
a towel in her hair.

She wraps her fresh sari
around her damp body.

Time to light the vilakku
begin to unfold
the neatly pressed day.

Laundry

I've taken my clothes
from your house
and as I dress, I find
in the careful creases
our mislaid friendship
where you folded it
between layers
of well-loved fabric.

Cool Comfort

Sleeping on cement
straw covered
paai shaped comfort.

A morning mat rolled up
and tiredness with it
out of sight.

The essence of sleep
surface, softness, silence,
paai, pillow, peace.

Kollam

Rising at dawn to bathe and pray
she joins kollam dots
because they look beautiful that way.

At night no need to say
what will tomorrow bring
rising at dawn to bathe and pray.

She does not wish for the days
to be her own, she thinks
they look beautiful this way.

Festival, weekend or week day
the routine is the same
rising at dawn to bathe and pray.

Late night row, the pain lasts all day
her mother advises her to adjust
she'll look beautiful that way.

She has no place to hide away
and this is what women do
rise at dawn to bathe and pray
because they look beautiful that way.

Malayali Moon

The crescent moon cups the darkness
I wait for the sadness to overflow
instead sliver fills to circle
transforming pain to light
the circumference melts
evaporating in a misty cloud
poornima shrinks to amavasai
and I am left in darkness.

Deepawali

small diyas on broken stone walls
flickering in the crisp night
stars and flames alone
against the darkness

load shedding in operation
power company shirking its duty
allowing oceans of light on main streets
shops hidden behind curtains of yellow bulbs
luring money, igniting passion

outside the golden circle
the dark cold embraces
the diyas die down
cold and still they sleep

Annapurna Villas

the lovers sit on a moonlit balcony
eating bread and cheese with wine
and olives, enjoying the balmy evening

below the street sleeps in fits
mosque counting hours
to the next prayer call
children lying hungry on bare floors
plagued by mosquitoes
smell of raw sewage wafts up
street dogs fight over a stale chapatti
neighbours tremble at the thought
of such impropriety

this girl is trying to conjure
a Mediterranean scene in South Asia
but first she must learn the language
Hindi or Urdu works well here
djinn left over from the Mughal times
may understand and help
create a protective bubble
around this soft romantic scene

Lizard

The colourless woman slipper slaps on steps
key hard in the lock, door opens, fan's switched on.
The world turns, for a moment I fly, blink of her eye,
slap the floor and four feet foot it fast away.

'Pardesi Jaana Nahin'

movie in four scenes
setting: crowded Katra market

scene i

he whips out his pocket comb
neatly coiffs his hair
in a double handed gesture
begins his song, a star role
he's proud of

scene ii

she hears the song
catchy tune, unaware
her fate is sealed
by these singing lips
trapped between the bars

scene iii

hustling bodies
hooting horns
constant surveillance
curious eyes, any slowness
an invitation to conversation

scene iv

later she understands
the words, the tune
her part, the script
she feels type cast
but cannot find a better role

Allahabadi Sonnets

i

She's lying on a bed. To her left the balcony
    where she tried to be French, dragged table
and chairs, served cheese and wine, but neighbours'
    stares, sewer stench, pressure cooker whistles,
the evening bhajans, did not ring true.
    Propped by pillows she can see the smaller balcony,
from there grassy patches after rains,
    the derelict school, where well paid teachers
and working children never show, the dhobi
    hangs his dry cleaning on the hedges,
evening the muezzin sings and the doodh wallah
    calls his cow ao ao ao as he cycles by.
She is silenced by the flood of sound, her words
    never moving beyond breath.

ii

Eyes strip her naked as she passes
    the ration shop queue. Back home,
lizard slaps to the floor as the fan starts
    to turn. She hides behind a lattice of books
stacked by the bed, seeking a story
    to tell herself. The old tale of a lonely child
surrounded by horses, dogs and fields
    will not work, time and place have shifted.
She reads Mahfouz, in Cairo finds the early morning
    muezzin, the cool darkened rooms and balconies
of Allahabad. Is she the wife, the other woman?
    There are no bells, there is no ring and neighbours
have complained. Her dream was of the title role
    in the movie of her life but this is just a walk on part.

iii

The silence in her head is crazy making,
    she can't be sure she is, feels a fading
sense of self. Only a story on a page
    can save her and so she sits to write.
She knows the bhajans by heart, can cook
    for two on a one ring stove, can count
the whistles for the rice and dal. There's
    not much to say, no story to be told.
Her news is of buying stamps, discovering
    a wasteland only to realise it is an open air
toilet, meeting women who see in her
    an escape from their dreary lives.
She writes long letters home, to be shared.
    Her father urges caution.

iv

Each weekend the paperwallah comes
    he buys the unwanted copies, newspapers
and magazines, sells whole
    what will be read. Her pages
are ripped out, neatly folded into bags.
    In the pharmacy, her next supply of tablets
and tampons will come wrapped
    in her recycled words and empty pages.
Her silence encloses her, protects
    her modesty. She cannot be accused
of drawing attention or of telling truths
    she has been sworn to hide.
In Wheelers shop she searches out the words of naga women
    who shed all shame and proclaimed themselves.

v

Should she join the living nagi
   at Ardh Kumbh Mela, sit naked
before the paunchy police, enjoy
   the banter between them,
or silently observe, as a teacher
   is muted by a husband who speaks
roughly as his square fists tighten
   while another veils herself returning home
or listen to the girls bemoan the dearth
   of good boys, their angular
features, so clever and sharp
   unsoftened by romance or pleasure?
She learns to find joy in her love of him, with Rumi
   and bhakti she discovers god in the other.

vi

She maps that city with her feet
　　her tongue tastes each corner
Katra market potato fry in leaf kattori
　　cows patiently waiting their turn
mangoes of every shade and flavour
　　spread beneath leafy trees, warm
to the hand, Lengra's leather bound
　　sweetness lingers long on her tongue.
Walks Grand Trunk Road, a carnival of colourful trucks,
　　Ambassadors, Enfields, to reach Heera Halwai's and buy
creamy dahi and gulab jamun in hot syrup, ladled
　　from pan to clay pot, oozing through the pores.
She holds the touch of leaf and clay and skin
　　in her hand as the loo blows through her.

vii

She knows the tabla player, the dancer,
    the singer; women who make merry
on music. How they gather
    in each others' homes, trip
back and forth, their joy echoing
    between the buildings. One night
crossing the road to home, the singer
    is assaulted by thugs who pull
away her sari, under the watchful eyes
    of the chowkidar on either side.
They rush to the victim's aid
    when the goondas have moved off.
She learns that in these matters woman
    is all powerful, always to blame.

viii

Her movie star delivers ironed clothes
        weekly to her door. He uses a back-pocket comb
to fix his quiff before he knocks. She loves
        the warm touch of the freshly pressed cloth
the pleasure of an easy order on the shelf
        and one job less to do. The price per piece
is cheap. He returns the guards' uniforms
        with stiff creases, smart and smooth.
He asks the pandit guard for payment
        and receives it in lathi blows, so hard
they land him in hospital for weeks.
        But big men don't get fired, for fear.
When her movie star comes next
        his light has dimmed.

ix

When she tells the children tales
    of *grumpy balloon men, with fixed bunches,*
2,3,4 to stretch their number skills, *make five.*
    She sees two brothers sitting studying, rescued
from a mechanics workshop to learn
    ek, do, theen and a, aa, i, ee. And Rubina,
the girl child calculator, capable of adding
    up to five figures at a time, a skill learned
from selling vegetables on her parents' stall.
    And Shabnam who draws in black
her shadow world while her brother
    in all new clothes lives in technicolour.
Years later the brothers find her on MG Marg.
    They are selling balloons, one by one.

X

Dr Miss Ritu di has preserved their father's
    Cambridge China and bungalow.
She tells stories of dressing for balls
    and later of students with guns.
White ants eat her books while she feeds
    international strays. The teacher bent like
a question, married late, a cruel man
    rescued by her sisters, gently teaches
any child who wants to learn. And Dipu Aunty
    on her blue Honda scooter, behind her you are safe
from the goondas who attack village schools and rape
    the nuns. She runs a women's refuge, hard work her cure all.
They rescue her, mind her but she drifts away,
    she should return, she will, one day.

Old Katra, Allahabad

i

The name of the road has vanished from my mind. I google
to remember, find a news report from Katra Bazaar
where I did my shopping. A law student beaten to death
his leg had brushed against his attackers'. I watch Dilip Saroj
his chest bare, his body bent back on the pavement
as a man raises a brick to strike him again. The attacker
has political connections. The family received Rs 20 lakhs.

ii

For this Sarojini, you fought?

Dreams of delight that are gone,

...

And tender boughs flower on the plain

...

But what is their beauty to me, papeeha,

...

That brings not my lover again?

iii

Eram, named for a fantastical place
makes me tea in a lean-to kitchen
housewife to father, brother, uncle.

She dreams of escape, entrusts
to me her gold necklace and earrings

inlaid with stones, green and red.
Her innocence made her believe
that passion would not lead
her astray. Her mother compass'

absent, she's left her to find her way.
Eve, desperate for freedom
what did she find?

iv

a morning misted over
with a thick grey sky
a head of tasks
a knot of plans

beyond the clouds
a clear blue sky so thin
the branches of the red-bloomed
cotton tree pierce right through
to the market where I was serenaded—
the scene of a beating
now playing out
on YouTube

after Lal Ded's Vakhs, 38, 39

I was liquid carbon beneath the ocean,
the rot of ancient trees. They found
me, marked my location
from the heavens, then came
armed, exploding, drilling
through my carapace. They extracted
me and above the sea
they called me crude.
                I was taken by pipe
to be refined. They desire only my energy
all else is sludge to them and thrown
where it can only poison. Out of my element
I am deadly. I am used by industry,
                        turned
into synthetic fibre, but I remain petroleum
in my depths. They spin me into yarn and weave
and dye. Nameless engineers play artisan
with machines. They fabricate
material to be worn.
                I am wound
round woman's hips and she is heating oil.
My memory is stirred.
                    She suffers intense burns.
I am a twisted mess
melted to her skin.
                I long to return to my cool cave.

after Lal Ded's Vakhs, 88, 89

I enter the cage chain and whip in hands, I will tame
these thoughts, train them to perform tricks
on command, to obey me. At first they roar, so loud
I'm drowned in sound—no quiet space to crawl

away. I breathe. I calm my heart, it fights
to flee, my body aches with tiredness. I look
them in the eye, they swirl around and suck
me in, my soul has flown away. My whip I hold—

I've wrapped the lash around my chest from back
to front and through the loop and over shoulder
blades. I harness heartbeat, tie myself in knots—
but words are whistling round my head. I cannot think.

The rope is tightening fast, the distance between thoughts
a breath—

The Widow's Song

I put the flame
to your mouth
breathe peacefully

with one last look
I leave you
on the pyre

before sunset
I gather the ashes
and charred bones

store them
in a clay pot
and wait

when the wind
changes I'll
scatter them

upon the waves
free at last

Mehendi Artist

I spend my day
holding the hands
of countless strangers
squeezing henna
through cones to draw
patterns on the nameless
skins of women
who do not speak to me

they rest their hands
on my thigh and sit
close while I write
my dreams upon their palms
trace my fantasies
on their life lines

my designs will darken
and deepen overnight
lasting long after
the memory of my face

they squeeze lemon
to hold the design
to fix it fast

Sum kundera lay koti

he crouches ready
resting on haunches
bare feet grime-caked
outsize t-shirt
undersize shorts

when they go
he'll eat
soft hot idli
lapping up sambar

stomach tight
in shreds
like amma's saris
under his head
worn soft by her body
the bare walls
fling shouts at him
the hard fear
pushes him back
to work

Slap in a Staffroom

chopping ideas into
child-sized portions

phwish of paper
sliced with steel

bare feet slapping
on the stone floor

whisper of air slashed
my cry of pain

her laughter stained
with mosquito blood

open windows
report to all

violence lodged as flinch
deep in my body

The Coconut Seller

she raises her aruvaal to split the skull
of a green coconut, the customer waiting
to eat the cool white flesh and in that
instant a flash of memory

her son asleep on the stone step
cool in the hot afternoon, when they came
to disturb his peace, carrying the
same curved knives by which she lives
and her son died

she strikes the coconut and splits it on a stone
scrapes out the flesh and hands it over
waiting now for twenty rupees

Lakshmi Mittal in Zenica

I'd like to apologise
I'm here near to you
doing this dirty work

I make the metal which
suspends your lives
above reality

steel yourselves
I will not filter
the truth of pollution

I would be in India
where you can, more easily
ignore my dirty work

but here is nearer
all the easier
to reach you, less dear

my workers bend regulations
like reinforcement bars
precast postponed promises suffice

the limit cannot be exceeded
without measure, there is no data
it's my pleasure

I fulfil your need
make your dreams reality
I'm here near you

I am a blend
of sweetness and steel
mithai and metal

I'm here and I'm near
and I apologise for inconvenience
a child's asthma, an adult's death

I fulfil your need
bend legal steel
with my greed

you're trapped indoors for days
as my presence prowls the streets
heavy with minute metals

panting at the thought
of penetrating living bodies
planting my seed

feel my sweet strength
in the surgical steel reaping
a harvest of tumours

I'd like to apologise
for doing this dirty work
to fulfill your need

to satisfy my greed
I'm here near you

Googling Soni Sori

I looked for you online
your voice, your words, all I found
Who is responsible for my condition?

I read you're 35, three small children
left with family as you fled to Delhi
hoping for a chance to plea

your husband and nephew jailed
your father shot, your people
caught in the crossfire

no phone at home
it signals police informer
the only web you know a trap

arrested in Delhi
returned to Chhattisgarh
and there I found you

a two minute clip
wild haired moaning
cuffed to a hospital bed

I've found you tortured
and broken—your words
ring in my head

Who is responsible for my condition?

Sathya Sutra

i.m. Isaipriya and the many others, Mullivaikal 2009

it is in the details
put side by side by side
that we find the truth
the whole picture
sharp and clear

each stitch tight and well angled
the needle pierces the fabric
sharp and well-aimed

I know the truth of genocide
is not in the numbers
raped or murdered or displaced
each swollen body is a stitch
in the rough red fabric
part of the whole

the newsreader in her yellow sari
her image on the screen glowing
later reduced to grainy footage
of a partially clothed corpse
on the back of a garbage truck

the frightened faces of the children
forbidden to approach amma's body

the planes will return to bomb
the rescuers—the adults know

and there are those who will unstitch
these knots, attempt to destroy the pattern
but look, here, see the scraps of thread
remaining, holes where once the stitches were

more evidence has come

uniform rape recorded
on phones, by individuals
beside their family photos
women stripped naked
reduced to carcasses
with remnants
of their humanity
clinging on

these words should name you
speak of your life
what you did for the years
before your death
the discussions you had
the meals you cooked and ate
the clothes you washed and wore
the books you read
the people you loved
the touches you gave
the hugs you received

but I do not know the details
I have no name, no age
the evidence has been destroyed
all that remains is your body
bare and broken
on my screen

the smirks and bared teeth
of camouflaged soldiers
doing their *duty*
in the jungle
before returning
to their families

Ghazal for Parveena and her son, Javaid (disappeared, 1991)

Where have you hidden my new crescent moon?
I search for my son by the light of the moon

A hawk swooped down and took him away
is he high in the mountains, near to the moon?

When he disappeared my fear went away
I approach the armed men under sun and moon.

I've searched camps, hospitals and jails
where is he? Can my child see the moon?

I watched over my son as he grew
under the waxing and waning of the moon.

The bodies they've found prove our worst fears
the tears of the living light up the moon.

I cannot forget his bright sunny face
grey corpses glitter beneath the full moon.

Ghazal for a Kashmiri Girl

In a small town a teenage girl comes out
dishevelled from a stinking bathroom, considered out

of bounds—and they argue about decency
and question her honour. Out

of bounds to query the soldier who
also emerged after she came out.

The witnesses gathered a crowd
went to the barracks and called him out.

He never came but she was held with
her father, her aunt— all kept out

of their home for days.
until a police video was put out

it was all nothing, nothing happened. Five locals
died, before the news of nothing got out.

Ghazal for Asifa

I look up her name, Asifa
this eight year old girl, Asifa

standing there with her horse
watching the family herd. Asifa

means one who brings people together.
These men took a girl, Asifa

tortured her with their hate
rape, murder, adult crimes against Asifa.

Destroyed the temple of her. Aziza,
Azadi, Farhana, I wish for Asifa.

Family fled in fear with their horses.
Could they even bury Asifa?

Now fear in the hills, and no horses
with a bright watchful child, Asifa.

Mary and Sunil

after 'My Unusual Grandparents', by Tanith Carey

I have headed east
from Haverfordwest
left behind my child
my shame, myself

> I headed west
> from East Pakistan
> my caste and pride
> erased by Kala Pani

sangam, sacred place of meeting
water, two colours
flowing side by side
through mountain ridges

> To earn a living
> I mass produce
> vinegar
> with all my Vedic
> learning

> and now these Britishers
> sprinkle my water
> on their chips

> before eating
> my father adjusts

his sacred thread
and pouring water
in his hand
mumbling a prayer
sprinkles it around his food

the essence of all beings is the earth
the essence of the earth is water

This man I do not understand
has given me three children
I could not have conceived

they are mine
but what am I?
no roots here,
no twisting lanes
winding around green hills
surrounded by high rise
they speak with London air
in their lungs

the essence of man is speech
the essence of woman breath
when the two come together
they fulfil each other's desire

My children will never
see a Durga Puja
never know the taste of mishti doi
dance before the Goddess Kali

bearing incense on the beach
the drum beats
building up and up
until the only way is seaward
and the Goddess must be drowned

and I was drowned
when I crossed the Kala Pani

let there be no quarrel between us
let us learn together in harmony
let there be peace

Fever

they're right
dengue is biphasic
it's struck again
days on end
confined to bed
delirious
resistance is low
I'm weak and unresolved
scared of the future
where platelets drop
and body melting
I die

Mattancherry Window

misnamed the Dutch Palace
wallowing in damp green
with water buffaloes

courtyard a wooden temple
sacred fire open only to men
unstitched, half bare

shaded inside the artists' passion
in Kathakali colours
burnished clinging to the walls

that languid grin
Krishna and his gopis
his fingers pluck a ripe
nipple, plump female flesh

through wooden slats
there is the tank
cool in the midday heat

shadowed by trees
dappled water
cool and still

Fióna Bolger

after Mahadeviyakaa

oh night soft with jasmine
moon full to overflowing
tiles holding the last heat
from the day's warmth
our soles rubbed red
we sprawl on straw mats
we've come together to eat

oh night heavy with jasmine
should I praise the joining
or the separation
the dull peace
or the painful consciousness

they've changed the tiles
they look the same
we never sit there now
we never sit
we never
we
are no more

oh night full with memories
distant stars I can never reach
you are maya
tugging on my plait
turning my head

Boomerang in Kovalam

The waves pulling the sand back
clear the marks you've made. You dig
your heels into the wet sand again
and watch the water pull sand away
suck you in. Let us record this
you and me on a beach
watching the ocean waves
feeling the shift of the earth beneath us.

We can replay it for days
and weeks to come.

Your almost adult foot, your still childish
excitement, again and again, let us play
let us play every day, and week, and year
and pray we'll play together ever after.

Viewpoint

I want to locate my vanishing point
where all lines are held, everything brought
into perspective. When I unroll the child's
brown-paper drawing of East Coast Road, sideways
cars, autos, cycles, it is longer than the gods'
journey, festival chariots pulled through the streets
and I see the vanishing points are multiple
and drag me into silence.

Calculating

Bike ride on an Enfield, to stand
in line with ladies for a man
too lazy to join the men's queue, willing
to use any woman to get what he wanted.

I am twice humiliated, his rudeness
and my later scolding. My calculations
were awry. Next time I am more careful
with my figures.

My daughter has found touch-me-nots
in the park, they curl away from her small digits.

Golu Dolls

lying in their cardboard boxes
wrapped in newspapers
they can hear the sounds outside
feel the slight chill in the air
the season has come

time for them to be arranged
on steps in all their glory
for visitors to come and see
sing, dance, share sundal
but nothing—no one comes

A Sumeet Mixie Box of Photos

it's time to leave our home
the wardrobe packed full of photographs

mountains you climbed in Polish miners' boots
soles later ripped off and replaced

deserts where we slept under Holi moons
heard of a birth far away

days by the sea, building sand temples
fully dressed splashing in the waves

and then our wedding album
three days of joining together

bound so tight we felt choked

and when I struggled to be free
you held on tighter

the mixie is still working
but not for me

By Halves

We three crossed East Coast Road then it was still one and a half lanes each side.

She must have been in his arms, she was two and a half.

There was no space to walk with cycles and bikes sharing the half path

and the photo shop wasn't so old fashioned, it was half renovated.

They couldn't find a tacky alpine backdrop or plastic flower prop, we did it by half,

a green cloudy screen and she squeezed our heads to hers, fully hers she does nothing by halves

after that we were no longer one but two halves and she was in between.

'My head speaks English but if my limbs could speak,
they'd speak Malayalam.'

after Jijo Sebastian

I remember how dumb
I was, trying to speak Irish
to my daughter for a month
instead remaining silent

speechless, listening to her father
babble river stream of words
mudhu muri, muddamma,
bangara magoo, putani muri

my love, deserted by sound
burned hot inside me until
I spoke with limbs, the language
of cells, then came these words

I do not dare to call my own
stolen from another land
copied from another mother

Cut and Paste

I tore the child away
ripped along the dotted lines
and in my haste
I left the edges frayed

I put her on a different page
of our world atlas
not a random choice
my place of origin

and now she's blended
the edges evened out
like a chameleon
she's faded into the background

shall I tear her out again
and using Fevicol
attempt to paste her back
where once she belonged

Unbalanced

she climbs the terrace steps
ascends to view the overarching dome
escapes a squared off room, rectangled window
to see the roundness of the sky above

but from the terrace, buildings jut
and spike, horizon's gone
the sea, a small semi-circle caught
between apartments, clouds curve

and bend evening light to reddish shade
round beaked parrots cut through the air above
flock formation slips through the sky
escaping for a time the grounding lines

From Lakshmi's Balcony

workers' shouts
shook gravel
metal scratching concrete
diesel engine chugs
all ground into the mix
of an afternoon

building rises
clears trees
approaches the sun
wealth evaporates
before it can trickle down
ground water depleted

salty brine is all that remains
in this concrete world

G5 Block V, Shivani Apartments

Balcony to balcony, terrace to terrace we want to swing, float
above the sweating city. Everyone is reaching high
to catch the breeze. A glance from the kitchen used to be
blue now grey, no longer sky, turned plaster wall, dull

blocking our eyes' escape to the sea, and koel and crow
close up black and shining. Who returns to the us in shadow
form? The nest just beyond our reach a merry jumble.
I have been given these hours, these hot humid hours

clock ticks, crow squawks and autos chug in the distance
the thud of wet cloth on stone, the swish of thodapam
on clay, the sleepy cry silenced in the building across
an impatient driver sets up a rat tat tat, pressure cooker

whistle on the building's other side, the wave of a seller's
call sends ripples through the air and I sit silent and still

Rasika III

sitting on her bed
propped up with pillows
holding court
her women around her

explaining the scoring
on Australian Master Chef
she wants the boy to win
his mother struggled so hard

on the balcony puzzling
over half dead plants
rejoicing at a single jasmine bud
about to bloom

at a concert, wearing sari
fingers looped around the raga
pulling the music around us
wrapping us in sound

concocter of pepper rasam
maker of ven pongal, chakara pongal
pickle lady to some
feeder of friends, flood victims, all

conjuror of connections
gatherer of friends
rasika of life

Chakra

Ashoka's wheel spins
through history, stone
carved symbol,
spinning wheel,
cycle wheel.

I feel freedom on two wheels—
at speed you can outrun the heat
for a short time but when you stop
she catches you and then revenge is hers.

As I stand astride my cycle enforcing the red light
on impatient truck traffic I hear the copper coin click
of peepal leaves over the wayside altar, roadside temple.
Shrine to the hope of people that something may change.
The trishul stands, three lemons
sharp and bitter, pierced by its prongs.

Lights turn green, I move off, keeping to the edge as trucks speed
by, boy banging the side to scare pedestrians, dogs, cows, cyclists.
Motor bikes weave in and out, blue bottles, never quite there when
the vehicles close in.

In this procession we travel past the temple
where side by side women will cook dal rice
over wood fires. But that is January and it is July.
We eat ven pongal and chakara pongal to remind us
of the fresh village of the harvest festival

when we will be far away. No chance to sit
before the temple, light our kindling
and let the goodness overflow before the morning sun.
The biryani of Eid has been cooked, shared and enjoyed
and we are celebrating the joy of rice and dal.

My daughter discovers
India's ancient kings: Muslim and Buddhist and Hindu. A past fast
being buried by a saffron bound vision of the future. This history
not destined for school books but burned in a pyre on which the
living dissenter may also be burned.

Kathri poo neeram,
a sari the colour of the flower
of the aubergine plant.

Kathrikai podi, soft, spicy, sweet
as a cotton handloom podhivai
in strands of wind spun
on a cycle wheel, woven
into an afternoon sea breeze,
floating on my skin.

Blunt Knives

i

Words are my gold and you
handed me so many they weighed
me down. I fingered my new found
wealth until you packed up
your illusion, went away
leaving nothing behind.
The coins turned copper, medicinal
metal, a cure for vanity and believing
beautiful untruths.

ii

Master of the visual
you bend words
like light they enter
my brain upside down.
I've no way to right them.

I misread them, miss
red them, I miss
green mango
patterned saris,
the rejoicing soil
after agni nakshetram,

the star which burns
everything to red

iron rich, while the poor
are anaemic, the rich
have no backbone.

iii

And the frogs emerge rejoicing
in the dampness, they are everywhere
but where your foot lands. They live
avoiding falling feet.

iv

My feet fall mainly in my mouth as I attempt to drill through stone
with my teeth.

v

The carpet is pure wool,
duck egg blue the waiting room
a dentist's surgery where I
went to confess my teeth
enumerate my sins, late nights
rushed mornings unloved
gums and missing fillings
There are gaps filled
with emptiness, it leaks out
pools in crevices and fissures.

vi

Your skin touching mine draws tear marks on my cheeks
 I clench my eyes making a fist of this moment

vii

Butter straight from the fridge is too hard to spread. It makes
crackers break and puts holes in sliced pan. In boarding school we
mashed butter on the side of the bowl to soften it. This was how
young ladies behaved at afternoon tea. Our box pleats carried butter
and jam stains from knives wiped on formica table edges. The knives
were blunt but there were other sharp edges. You learned to turn
your back to protect major arteries.

viii

skin taught to sing
kanjira, mrindagam
tha hata juma theri thaak
skin of sole to temple stone
thay ditha thay, thay thay ditha thay
skin pours itself into the rhythm
thay thay thay ditha thay
jasmine scented sweat

ix

The wind is an instrument, sailors
play well, inflates the fantasy
carries carpets over waves.
Magical thinking, a science
not yet explained

x

'Somewhere someone is traveling furiously toward you,'

xii

smaller than a bee, in the rain cloud
forest, bright frogs are found
their colours shout, 'touch me not'

women's black burqas
shed as they fled the darkness of eye-es
reveal shifting silken shades
glow ahmar, burtaqali, asfar,
akhdar, azraq, nili, argwani.

xiii

With every word she spoke, golden coins fell from her lips because
she had been gentle and kind to the baby crocodile. Her cruel sister's
every breath released a shower of frogs from her mouth in payment
for her harsh treatment of the little one.

xiv

Today I gave my green away, frittered the gold on idle objects
and now I feel more see through, waves of light flow
between my ribs and my stomach churns with the breeze
of movement. I want to reach a point of stillness, each shade
and time fixed, the sun no longer changing everything
moment to moment, the moon unable to work a glistening
magic on the dull of days. I wish to be a stillness which has seeped
into the air and is almost, just almost, not there.

Flying South

I come in July and bring
rain to cool the parched ground
mangoes still hang green, lie
orange, glowing in the market.
I will eat my fill. I do not deserve
the cooling rain, the mango
sweetness. My body
has been wrapped in Irish sun
strawberries and raspberries
have reddened my lips.

Wapas

I am returning
to the cloudy sky
promising rain

I am returning
to the woman who walks
at five to avoid—

I am returning
to the scratching
grabbing crows

I am returning
to the horns
charging down the ECR

I am returning
to the sea breeze
which cannot be bought or sold

I am returning
to the death place
of romance

I am returning
to the birthplace
of understanding and my daughter

I am returning
always and forever
returning and returning

The Middle of April

after Robert Hass

i

whan that Aprill with his shoures soote
the droghte of March hath perced to the roote
my grandfather quotes
Chaucer from the vinyl

ii

he knows more now
we will too soon

iii

in the spring
pelmet of green

in the summer
scarf of orange

in the autumn
shawl of white

iv

bamboos knock out a tune
until disturbed by elephants
grazing, discarding as they go

v

The dangers lie in the jugular. No one really likes the smell of elephant poo but it makes paper of a high quality. Words written on digested bamboo. Nothing is lost between page and palm. That is mystery: pen, ink, paper, thread, card, dream, word. A memory clings like the smell of dung. And there are always fibres.

vi

let there be peace between us
let us learn together
om santhi santhi santhi

vii

there's no shit like
your own shit

viii

And instead of entering the reserve forest we wandered through the village. The tea shop sold weak milky tea. We heard them, small black cows with bells around their necks. People warned us an elephant herd was nearby. We found their still steaming dung. This was all free and unreserved.

ix

the green mango is sour
best eaten karam with vellum

Nagpur loose jackets are rare now
orange trees cut to grow apartments

the iron red soil of Niyamgiri
woven into the shawl

x

Here are some things to eat from a banana leaf: idli, dosa, uttapam,
appam, idiappam, sambhar, rasam, chutney, chutney podi,
kozhikattai, thair saddam, thokku, chappatti, parotta, puri, anna
saru, chakhra pongal, ven pongal. Ungaishtam sapdingo.... Eat
your desire.

xi

still searching
for the man in the cafe

xii

silk saree

xiii

she said: ask them
and he said: no
she said: why is it
like this?
he said: nothing
she said: no
he said:

xiv

theyn kuricha nari
the fox who has drunk honey

xv

and from vinyl I learned
He loves you, yeah, yeah...
Did you happen to see...
myself in those songs?

xvi

agni nakshetram—
water tastes sweet
as mango juice trickles
from finger tip to hand
to elbow and bathed every veyne
in swich licour, of which vertu
engendered is the flour

'A foreigner is someone who makes us feel we belong'

after Amitava Kumar

I have never belonged
I am the foreigner
for so many people
the outsider
the unknown

that is me.

Pardesi, pardesi jaana nahin
Mujhe chhod ke, mujhe chhod ke

My fate sealed by these singing lips
trapped between these bars.
Firangi, but a friendly firangi
a lal didi, a pumpkin head
a vellai kari, one slight stress
removed from servant maid.
Difference noted, acknowledeged
appreciated, mostly ignored.

Returning to my native place
birth place—expecting blending
acceptance, receiving jarring
sensation of difference,
fractured self not of the place
but native to it.

Fióna Bolger

I find myself masala
of somewhere else
fitting but fractured
blending and bonding
but without roots
taking hold and digging deep.

Desi or pardesi
immigrant or emigrant
indigenous or disingenuous
pretending or blending
deceiving or conceiving
another way, elsewhere
anywhere, but here.

In and Out of Never Never Land

i.m. Maeve Brennan

The click of the heater
switching on and off
regulating temperature

peels of laughter
overflowing from a book
spilling down the stairs to me

cars accelerate up the hill
pause at the top, turn
and fade to silence

      the clock on summer time
      counts the seconds
      it proves winter will end

      I'm here now on winter time
      snow moments, icy seconds
      next week sunny hours will slide by

            fans will turn and mosquitoes
            hum the dusk hour's approach
            my time will stretch

            lazy mornings will begin leisurely
            kitchen clatter and daughter chatter
            ignored as I roll over for another hour

traffic streaming south
a constant drone
horn punctuated

until return flight
drops me back
in this snow silenced world

where we are frozen
but time moves faster
forcing me forward

I cannot keep up
out of step I trudge
behind my peers

NOTES

a compound of words

This poem was written in a Jo Shapcott workshop.
Wajalukinat: Dublin slang for 'What are you looking at?'
Saala: Literally means brother- in- law in Hindi, but can be a term of affection or an insult.
Aadivanga knee: In Chennai this slang means 'do you want a slap?'
To 'cruise for a bruise' means the same thing in Dublin.

Pattambuchi

Pattambuchi: The Tamil word for a butterfly is 'pattambuchi'. 'Pattam' means kite and 'puchi' means insect.

Rasika I

Rasa means the essence of something.
A rasika is being someone who can appreciate and savour that essence.

View through the Crack

Khoa: It is made from milk thickened by heating in an open iron pan.

Oranges are not the only fruit

The title *Oranges Are Not the Only Fruit* by Jeanette Winterson reprinted by permission of Peters Fraser & Dunlop on behalf of Jeanette Winterson.

Lengra, Alphonso and Banganapalli are all mango varieties.

Words to a New Wife Entering her Kitchen

Manjal: Turmeric
Levang: Cloves
Jeera: Cumin
Saunf: Fennel
Menthia: Fenugreek
Ghusa Ghusa: Poppyseed
Raw mangoes: Unripe mangoes
Maambaram: It means ripe mangoes.

Aubade

Vilakku: Diya or oil lamps.

Cool Comfort

Paai: Dry grass mat.

Kollam

Kollam are rice flour or chalk geometric patterns drawn by women at their front doors morning and evening in some south Indian communities.

'Pardesi Jaana Nahin'

Title of a song from *Raja Hindustani*, 1996. It translates to 'foreigner, don't leave me'.

Malayali Moon

Poornima: Full moon
Amavasai: No moon

Allahabadi Sonnets

Bhajans: Sacred songs in Hindu tradition.
Doodh wallah: A man who sells milk.
Dhobi: Person who washes, dries and irons clothes for others.
Naga: Naked
Nagi women: Naked holy women.
Kattori: Bowl
Dahi: Yoghurt
Loo: A hot dust laden wind in north India.

Old Katra, Allahabad

The quoted lines are from 'A Love Song from the North', by
Sarojini Naidu.
Eram: Eden

after Lal Ded's Vakhs

These poems were inspired by Vakh's (sayings) from *I, Lalla: The
Poems of Lal Ded*, translated by Ranjit Hoskote, Penguin Classics,
2013.

Sum kundera lay koti

A phrase in Kannada meaning 'sit down and shut up you monkey'.

The Coconut Seller

Aruvaal: The curved knife used for cutting coconuts.

Lakshmi Mittal in Zenica

This poem was inspired by Esad Hesamovic's article, 'Dying of
Pollution in Zenica'. Available at: http://www.balcanicaucaso.org/

eng/Regions-and-countries/Bosnia-and-Herzegovina/Dying-of-pollution-in-Zenica-125737

Sathya Sutra

Sathya Sutra: The thread of truth

Mary and Sunil

The poem was inspired by the following article https://www.theguardian.com/lifeandstyle/2010/jul/10/readers-favourite-photographs-songs-recipes
Mishti doi: Sweet curd; a Bengali delicacy.
Kala Pani: Literally means the black water. It was believed by some that crossing the sea erased caste and community ties.

Boomerang in Kovalam

Boomerang is a feature on some social media apps which allows repeated playing of a short video clip.

Calculating

Touch-me-nots: A plant with leaves which close up when you touch them.

Golu Dolls

Golu dolls: A Tamil Brahmin tradition of setting up steps of ornamental dolls and statues in the home during the Dussehra festival.
Sundal: A boiled chickpea snack with fried chilli, lemon juice, coconut and curry leaves.

'My head speaks English but if my limbs could speak, they'd speak Malayalam.'

Mudhu muri, muddamma, bangara magoo, putani muri are Kannada pet words for a child translating to sweet baby, pet, beautiful baby, tiny little one.

Cut and Paste

Fevicol: A popular brand of glue in South Asia.

G5 Block V, Shivani Apartments

Thodapam: Sweeping brush made from grasses or twigs.

Rasika III

Ven Pongal: Savoury rice and moong dal dish.
Chakara Pongal: Sweet rice and moong dal dish.

Chakra

Kathri poo neeram: The colour of the flower of the brinjal (aubergine) plant.
Kathrikai podi: A dish made of brinjal fried in a spicy powder.
Podhivai: Sari.

Blunt Knives

Agni nakshetram: The fiery star which is visible in the last two weeks of May, the hottest time of the year in Tamil Nadu.
Kanjira: A small South Indian drum.
Mridangam: A large South Indian drum.
Stanza viii: These are rhythms and words to denote rhythms, nattawangam.

'Somewhere someone is traveling furiously toward you …' has been taken from 'North Farm' by John Ashbury.
The following are the rainbow of colours in Arabic.
Ahmar: Red
Burtaqali: Orange
Asfar: Yellow
Akhdar: Green
Azraq: Blue
Nili: Indigo
Argwani: Purple

Wapas

Wapas: To return

'A foreigner is someone who makes us feel we belong'

Vellai kari: A white person.

The Middle of April

Written during a Mimi Khalvati workshop, structure borrowed from 'The Beginning of September', by Robert Hass.

Quotes at the start and end are from Chaucer's 'Prologue to the Canterbury Tales'.
Karam: Spicy.
Vellum: Boiled and hardened sugar cane juice.

In and Out of Never Never Land

The title has been taken from Maeve Brennan's first collection of short stories published in 1969, US.

FIRST PUBLICATION CREDITS

Sathya Sutra and extracts from Blunt Knives were first published in *Triptych*, Poetry Bus Press, April 2019.

a compound of words was first published in *Wretched Strangers*, Boiler House Press, June 2018.

The Mehendi Artist was first published in *Flare*, Issue 6, February, 2018.

Extracts from Allahabadi Sonnets were first published in *All the Worlds Between*, Yoda Press, 2017.

The Coconut Seller was first published in *Flare*, Issue 5, October 2017.

The Middle of April was first published on *Poethead*, 2014.

Oranges are not the only fruit, Mattancherry Window, The Widow's Song, View through the Crack were first published in *The Geometry of Love Between the Elements*, Poetry Bus Press, 2013.

Off Course was first published in *Barehands*, Issue 9, 2013.

In and Out of Never Never Land was first published in *The Poetry Bus*, Issue 4, 2013.

'Pardesi Jaana Nahin' and Cut and Paste were first published on *The Brown Critique*, 2012.

Malayali Moon was first published in *The Mews*, Airfield Writers, June 2012.

Words to a New Wife, Pattambuchi and Mary and Sunil were first published on *The Brown Critique*, 2010.